GROWING
IN FAITH

GROWING IN FAITH

• • •

CHARLES F. STANLEY

VICTOR BOOKS

A DIVISION OF SCRIPTURE PRESS PUBLICATIONS INC.
USA CANADA ENGLAND

If you have ever visited a museum or special historical exhibit, you probably saw pictures and paintings of famous people from the past who did great things for the world and for society. There they are, with a name-plate or plaque describing what they did, for generations of onlookers to appreciate and remember.

Try to imagine the display if the great heroes of faith from the Bible had a special place in a museum. You would see a picture of Noah, building an ark just because God told him to, in spite of the mocking onlookers. You'd see the image of Moses, lifting up his staff and stretching out his hand over the Red Sea, so that God would part the waters for the fleeing Israelites. Joseph would be on the wall too the one who trusted God to deliver him after his brothers sold him into slavery as a young man.

The portrait of Samson would show him pushing down the pillars of the Philistine house, when God gave him back his strength. The Prophet Elijah would be in the middle of his dramatic showdown with the prophets of Baal. Ruth's picture would capture the moment when she told her mother-in-law Naomi she would follow her God and stay by her side. King David's picture would show a young boy standing before the mighty, taunting giant Goliath.

The Apostle Peter would be standing in astonishment before the living Savior, exclaiming, "You are the Christ." And the picture of Stephen, the first believer to be martyred for his faith in Jesus, would highlight his gaze upward to heaven as the stones flew at his body.

Now try to imagine another picture next to all of these. It is down the hallway quite a bit farther, because the walls are filled up with people of faith of many years. It has the same kind of frame and a plaque with words underneath it. As you look closer, you realize you recognize the person in the portrait — it is you.

If you are startled at the thought that your picture could be hanging in the "hall of faith," you shouldn't be. You demonstrated faith the moment you trusted Jesus Christ to be your Savior and cleanse you from sin. You weren't relying on your own resources to try to please God, by attempting to work your way into His favor. In that time of humility and repentance before Him in prayer, you acknowledged that Christ and Christ alone was sufficient. You needed Jesus in order to have an eternal relationship with God, and by trusting Him for forgiveness, you took an incredible step of faith — faith that God gave you to enable you to trust Him with your soul and eternal destiny.

So What Is It?

It would probably be more helpful to begin with a brief description of what faith is not, given that there are many false definitions that can cause confusion.

Faith isn't just something for spiritual heroes or those of great renown. It is not a mysterious condition that "happens" to you. It is not a forced emotional or mental state or a contrived mind-set that admits only "positive thinking." Faith doesn't depend on your ability to manufacture feelings of confidence or joy. Faith isn't something that you need "more of" before you develop your relationship with the Lord. Faith isn't something that "impresses" God and therefore moves Him to do something for you.

Put very simply, faith is basic trust that God is who He says He is and that He will do what He promises in His Word. It may sound like too basic an explanation, but that is the heart of what it means to have faith in God. The following illustration has often been used to illustrate the difference between intellectual trust and real trust, or faith.

When you see a chair that looks sturdy, you have no problem sitting in it. As you place your weight on the seat and actually sit in the chair, you are essentially *trusting* that chair with your body. If you only *say* that the chair can hold you, but you never sit in it, you are not trusting yourself to the care of that chair. Though this comparison is limited in many respects, you could say that faith is believing the chair will support you at the same time that you physically let it support you.

God's Word gives His definition of faith. Hebrews 11:1 says, "Now faith is the assurance of things hoped for, the conviction of things not seen." Even though you cannot perceive spiritual truths with your physical senses, you know within your spirit that they are real because God says they are. God takes your trust in Him and grows it, nurturing it day by day. As time passes and you enjoy an intimate relationship with the Lord, and as you see how He operates in your daily life, your trust in Him and His faithfulness to you solidifies.

This process is often referred to as a strengthening of your faith. Through a living experience of fellowship with God, you come to depend and rely on Him with your entire being. That is genuine faith, and that is what motivated the great characters of the Bible. If faith depended on how much we could give to God, then no one would have faith. Moses didn't stand before the Pharaoh of Egypt because he believed he would perform well for God. He stood up and spoke before Pharaoh because God gave him the power and ability.

When you read the stories of Old Testament heroes, you discover that many were powerless or poor or unskilled when God laid His hand on their lives. They became His instruments to do mighty works as they trusted Him to do the job; they were weak people with a strong God.

Why Should I Trust God?

When you follow any kind of leader, one of your first concerns is that person's trustworthiness. A leader who vacillates randomly in making decisions or who in general demonstrates poor character is not someone you feel comfortable following. If you are going to walk side by side with someone and pursue his goals as your own, then that person must be worthy of such trust.

Human leaders always fall short of the ideal, but God never does. He is holy, righteous, omnipotent, omniscient, eternal, and perfectly loving. First Timothy 6:15-16 describes the Lord this way: "God, the blessed and only Ruler, the King of kings and Lord of lords, who alone is immortal and who lives in unapproachable light, whom no one has seen or can see." (NIV)

The God who created the entire universe out of nothing fashioned you personally. You are custom-made. He loves you unconditionally and has a plan for you, one that is good and satisfying and glorifying to Him (Psalm 139). You can trust Him with your life because He is your Maker. When you rest in His love and trust Him to do His work through you, you feel a significance and self-worth that cannot be taken away, and at the same time you become a channel of His blessing to others.

Have you ever had to take your car to a repair shop? Then you understand how it feels to wait for the mechanic to call and tell you what is wrong. Suppose when the call comes, the technician says that you need new brakes and a general tune-up.

At this point, you have to make a choice. You may either rely on the mechanic's word and have the work done, or you can take your car home. In most cases, you are probably going to have the repairs made. Why? You understand that the adjustments are for the benefit of the automobile. Without them, the car won't be able to operate at top efficiency, and it could be unsafe.

When God looks at your life, which He is carefully nurturing, He sees every detail with absolute precision. An auto mechanic can be in error about a car, but God is never wrong when it comes to knowing what is best for you. In all things He is working to conform you to the image of Jesus Christ and to prepare you for good works (Ephesians 2:10).

This character-building and guidance system are part of a step-by-step, gradual process. Along the way, God makes adjustments, either to keep you on track or to steer you in new directions. These changes might be minor, or they could be big and momentous. For example, the Lord could ask you to get rid of a personal habit or He might call you to change your entire career.

When the disciples were laboring with their nets at the Sea of Galilee, Peter and James and John had no concept of all the things that Jesus had in store for them. "[Jesus] saw two brothers, Simon who was called Peter, and Andrew his brother, casting a net into the sea; for they were fishermen. And He said to them, 'Follow Me, and I will make you fishers of men.' And they immediately left the nets, and followed Him." (Matthew 4:18-20)

No one knows for certain, but historical evidence and scriptural context tell us that these men were probably brought up in good Jewish homes. They had learned God's laws and heard His Word, but this was God as they had never known Him before. They could not anticipate the blessings and trials of the future, but they did know one thing: Jesus Christ was calling them to follow Him. And they obeyed.

As you mature in Christ, you discover one of your greatest difficulties is putting His instructions into practice. Whenever you sense

God directing you to make an adjustment to fit His purposes, you experience a critical turning point. Very often, God furnishes only what you need to know in order to make a decision. The future may appear fuzzy or incomprehensible from a human perspective, but He is not calling you to grasp the breadth and depth of His infinite wisdom. God wants you to trust Him completely and take the simple steps of obedience that He sets before you.

An All-Terrain Faith

If you have ever seen one of the new "all-terrain vehicles" that are so popular today, you were probably impressed with the tires. They are rugged and tough, and have treads that can grip any surface, from smooth asphalt to the grittiest of off-road trails. The tires are part of what make these vehicles so versatile; they can go anywhere they need to go because they are equipped with the right gear.

When you trust God to take care of you, you can be assured that He will equip you for the challenge. Circumstances that seem painful and confusing do not throw you off His chosen path because you know the Lord always uses the hurt to work out His special purposes in your life. In his book *Trusting God,* Jerry Bridges points out some of the spiritual problems that believers encounter when they go through a "smooth road" time:

"As difficult as it is to trust God in times of adversity, there are other times when it may be even more difficult to trust Him. These would be times when circumstances are going well, when, to use David's expression, 'The boundary lines have fallen . . . in pleasant places' (Psalm 16:6). During times of temporal blessings and prosperity, we are prone to put our trust in those blessings, or even worse, in ourselves as the providers of those blessings.

"During times of prosperity and favorable circumstances, we show our trust in God by acknowledging Him as the provider of all those blessings. . . . Soloman said, 'When times are good, be happy; but when times are bad, consider: God has made the one as well as the other' (Ecclesiastes 7:14). God makes the good times as well as the bad times. In adversity we tend to doubt God's fatherly care, but in prosperity we tend to forget it. If we are to trust God, we must acknowledge our dependence upon Him at all times. . . ."

Facing Life's Unknowns

Whenever circumstances change suddenly, especially when they change for what we perceive to be the worse, the shift may cause us to question where we're going. Whether you've been a believer for one month or one decade, it is easy to struggle with thoughts of doubt. Once again, this is the place where trust becomes the issue. The more "unexplainable" situations that you move through and then see God's provision as part of the larger picture, the less difficult it is to trust Him for the next crisis or heartache. This next story is a riveting example of something frightening and unknown turning into a reason for a lifetime of rejoicing.

As the pains of childbirth subsided, the woman held her new baby boy in her arms for the first time. She should have felt joy, but instead she felt a sickening knot forming in her heart.

She knew what the government had ordered her to do. The law said her baby boy must be killed immediately, just because he was a boy. But she also knew what Almighty God wanted her to do. Under the threat of death if she disobeyed, this mother made a decision. She said no to the evil law and yes to the Lord.

How was the woman Jochebed to know that one day God would use her boy Moses to deliver an entire nation out of Egyptian oppression? How could she possibly understand the eternal consequences of one action of faith? All she saw was a single choice, but because she perceived this trial through the eyes of faith, God turned defeat into hope for countless generations.

Maybe your life is peaceful, tranquil, and

predictable right now. You might even struggle with a little boredom or lack of motivation, since things are so mundane. You are reveling in a time of rest. But have you thought ahead to how you will react if bad news comes?

Let's say you're sitting around the house chatting with a next-door neighbor when the phone rings. The words you hear leave you stunned and speechless. You gasp. Your friend rushes to your side and says with a panicked voice, "What's wrong?" In one instant, the familiar, comfortable world you once took for granted feels blown to pieces, and you don't think those pieces will ever fit together again.

This scenario isn't presented to scare you or intimidate you into fear and anxiety about the future, but it is intended to help you consider the importance of absolute trust in God. Nothing is beyond His control. Nothing takes Him by surprise. And He promises to take the vilest situation and the most bitter tragedy and turn it into good for you. You can never read or meditate on the promise of Romans 8:28 too many times: "And we know that God causes all things to work together for good to those who love God, to those who are called according to His purpose."

Those who have not accepted Jesus as their Savior don't have a valid reason to "look on the bright side." The substance of our faith, the reality of our hope, is a living Savior who shed His blood to redeem you and give you an abundant life that begins now, in this life (John 10:10). Hebrews 6:19-20 says: "This hope we have as an anchor of the soul, a hope both sure and steadfast and one which enters within the veil [of God's presence], where Jesus has entered as a forerunner for us."

Faith Means Obedience

Almost eighty years after his mother Jochebed hid him from Pharaoh's men, a moment of decision came for Moses. He was out in the desert tending the family's sheep as he would on any other ordinary day. Then suddenly, he saw flames shooting upward, engulfing a bush without even singeing a single twig. It was not difficult for Moses to understand immediately that this scene was radically different from any one he had encountered before. Then in another moment of awe, God spoke from the fire.

God said: "Therefore, come now, and I will send you to Pharaoh, so that you may bring My people, the sons of Israel, out of Egypt" (Ex. 3:10). When Moses asked God what he should call Him, God replied, "I Am Who I Am" (v. 14).

God identified Himself as the eternal God who has no beginning or end. His character does not change. His purposes stand forever.

God was saying to Moses: "I am all-powerful, sovereign, and all-wise. I can take care of every problem. I have a plan. If you obey Me, you will find joy and fulfillment beyond imagination."

After the promises of God and the testimony of the past, wouldn't you think that Moses would have responded with a resounding "Yes, Lord!" His answer to God was less than enthusiastic: "What if they will not believe me, or listen to what I say?" (Ex. 4:1) Moses was filled with self-doubt and needless fear.

Have you ever been reluctant to trust God with confident faith, even though you know that He is able to do anything? Moses struggled with God for quite a while on this very issue. Finally, after the Lord countered every protest and refusal, Moses obeyed.

Look closely at what occurred when Moses recognized God's control over his life: he had a clearly defined mission and a reason for living. No matter what happened — and Moses would soon experience a lot of grief at the hands of an angry Pharaoh — he knew that God would see him through.

You can depend on the same absolute security as you submit your heart to the Lord. When you do yield to Him in faith, be prepared for some mighty transformations. You won't stay the same person for long; you'll become a person who sees life through the eyes of faith.

◆ *You view trials as opportunities.*

Before Moses know what God was up to, his long years in the desert as a fugitive from Egyptian law seemed a waste of valuable time. Yet when he glimpsed the future from God's perspective, the purpose became clear. During his desert years, God had quietly built into him solid leadership qualities, and the physical hardships gave him survival skills he would use later on the flight out of Egypt.

◆ *You desire obedience more than you want power or material wealth.*

Moses led a pampered life as the adopted son of the Pharaoh; it would have been easy for him to opt for a permanent life of ease rather than to take up the burdens of an oppressed people. You can learn the same lesson Moses did — it is not worth compromising and disobeying on "small" issues in order to secure money or avoid criticism from peers.

◆ *You see all of life in God's presence.*

All events are a part of God's blessing. The good and the bad play a role in His perfect pattern. Nothing can ruin your future. Your sure destination is the reason you do not have to give in to the deceit of feelings of despair or hopelessness.

When Moses' life was through, he had the joy of the knowledge that he came out a winner for one reason: he trusted God. Like all of us, he had times of questioning and anger and grumbling, but he learned the power of faith in the living God.

Moses was a risktaker, the kind God calls you to be in your walk with Him. In the book *Telling Yourself The Truth,* William Backus and Marie Chapian explain: "Faith itself is a risk. You must trust God and act in faith in order to take that step that you cannot see. If you're going to walk on water, you need to be willing to *take the chance* that you might sink to the bottom. . . .

"The misbelief that it is stupid or sinful to make decisions which might turn out wrong is unfounded. We're told to be wise as serpents, harmless as doves. Wisdom does not mean acting in fear or cowardice.

"Perfect love casts out fear means to us that the love of God has wiped out the power of fear over our lives if we will use God's methods of conquering it. 'Cast your fears [cares] on Me!' He explains. 'Give them to Me! I know what to do with them.' It is in this way that we are set free to take risks.

"Then whether we succeed or fail is not our utmost concern. We are not enslaved by fear of negative results. We willingly allow ourselves possible failure, possible negative results. . . .

"The Christian walking by the Spirit, in the will of God, can trust that outcomes of his actions in faith are totally in the hands of the Father. The truth for the Christian is that disaster, catastrophe, or utter defeat *cannot occur*. We have no business thinking in those terms! *God never fails.*"

Faith and Setting Goals

Some believers live in bondage to the idea that they cannot make decisions or plan ahead or look forward to the future because they do not know for certain what God has in store for them. The good news is that is not the way God designed faith to operate. God instilled within you the desire to work and plan and be forward-thinking; He wants you to anticipate His good plans for tomorrow.

Have you ever watched students in a graduation ceremony? You can see the thrilled expressions on their faces because they worked so diligently to get their diplomas. When the march is over, they shout for joy, leap up and down, and talk with eagerness together about where they are headed now.

That is how it feels to accomplish what you set out to do, and this feeling is wholesome. As a special workmanship in Christ, you are a new creation full of worth and potential

(Psalm 30:5; 2 Corinthians 5:17). God wants you to set specific goals based on His principles and to reach them through the strength He provides.

Goals are really a natural outgrowth of godly priorities, the things on which you place the most value. Your first activity in setting up a list of Christ-centered goals is to ensure that your priorities line up with God's. Matthew 6:33 says: "Seek first His kingdom and His righteousness; and all these things shall be added to you." God promises to fill your life with abundance as you learn to love Him first.

When your value system is confronted by the truth of Matthew 6:33, you are on the positive road to a godly understanding of what it means to have faith in God and set personal goals that fit His purposes. Ask yourself the following question: What does the Lord want me to do in the area of _____? You can fill in the blank with issues such as family life, finances, spiritual growth, the list is endless.

After you itemize the areas in which you feel God is leading you to take action, you're ready to build the kind of motivation that keeps you focused and on target. Writing down objectives is often helpful. In order to determine if your goals fit your walk of faith, submit the objectives on your list to the following criteria:

- *Will I be a better person?*
- *Does this goal mature me in Christ?*
- *Does this goal benefit others?*
- *Will others enjoy the rewards, too?*

If you can respond with a yes to these questions, you are headed in the right direction. A negative answer could signal a needed scriptural adjustment. Nothing is as refreshing as the satisfaction of knowing you are working for a God-given purpose.

You need to understand that walking by faith and striving toward Christ-centered goals is a process that may involve some occasional disappointments. But that does not mean that you are a failure or that somehow God has let you down. God's love has nothing to do with your performance.

Romans 8:35-39 says: "Who shall separate us from the love of Christ? Shall tribulation, or distress, or persecution, or famine, or nakedness, or peril, or sword? . . . But in all these things we overwhelmingly conquer through Him who loved us.

"For I am convinced that neither death, nor life, nor angels, nor principalities, nor things present, nor things to come, nor powers, nor height, nor depth, nor any other created thing, shall be able to separate us from the love of God, which is in Christ Jesus our Lord."

You cannot lose. Reaching out to strive toward a goal is always a good experience. When disappointment comes, you can treat it as a learning experience and keep on moving in wholehearted faith.

Genesis 24 tells a wonderful story of how faith and goals operate together. Abraham told his servant Eliezer to go into the land of his family to find a wife for Isaac, Abraham's son. The servant knew exactly what he needed to do, but he also knew that he could not get positive results through his own strength.

Before he went any farther, Eliezer prayed for God to grant him success. He then established an action plan in agreement with God's principles, trusting Him for completion. It wasn't very long before he arrived back home with Rebekah by his side. The real satisfaction of his adventure, and of yours as well, lies in seeing the Lord at work in your life. You are not alone in any endeavor. God promises to turn you in the direction you need to go at precisely the right time (Proverbs 16:9).

Do you desire to experience this type of satisfaction and joy? You can. You have everything to be excited about, especially in your relationship with a living and risen Savior who is bringing you into conformity to Him, working His will in your life until the day He brings you home to live with Him forever.

Isaiah 43:18-19 says: "Do not call to mind the former things, or ponder things of the past. Behold, I [God] will do something new, now it will spring forth; will you not be aware of it? I will even make a roadway in the wilderness, rivers in the desert."

Don't allow another day to pass without seeking God's plan for tomorrow and trusting Him to guide your feet along the path. You *are* somebody, because you have life through Christ and faith in a God who is perfect and holy and all-knowing. It is never too late to experience the awesome power of a God who loves you and desires to have one-on-one fellowship with you.